I want to be a Firefighter

Titles in this series:

WITHDRAWN
CHARLESTON COUNTY LIBRARY

I WANT TO BE A
Firefighter

DAN LIEBMAN

FIREFLY BOOKS

A Firefly Book

Published by Firefly Books Ltd. 2018

Copyright © 2018 Firefly Books Ltd.

All rights reserved. No part of this publication may be reproduced, stored in a retrieval system or transmitted in any form or by any means, electronic, mechanical, photocopying, recording or otherwise, without the written permission of the Publisher.

First Printing, 2018

Library of Congress Control Number: 2018934023

Library and Archives Canada Cataloguing in Publication
Liebman, Daniel, author
        I want to be a firefighter/ Dan Liebman.
Previously published: Willowdale, Ontario: Firefly Books, 1999.
ISBN 978-0-228-10097-3 (softcover).--ISBN 978-0-228-10142-0 (hardcover)
        1. Fire fighters--Juvenile literature. 2. Fire extinction--Vocational guidance--Juvenile literature. I. Title. II. Title: Firefighter.
TH9148 L53 2018   j363.37023   C2018-901012-6

Published in Canada by
Firefly Books Ltd.
50 Staples Avenue, Unit 1
Richmond Hill, Ontario L4B 0A7

Published in the United States by
Firefly Books (U.S.) Inc.
P.O. Box 1338, Ellicott Station
Buffalo, New York, USA 14205

Photo Credits:

© Drop of Light/Shutterstock.com, front cover
© TFoxFoto/Shutterstock.com, back cover, page 7
© blurAZ/Shutterstock, page 5
© Diane Garcia/Shutterstock, pages 6
© vicki/Shutterstock, pages 8–9
© Arisha Ray Singh/Shutterstock, page 10
© Prath/Shutterstock, page 11
© Nils Petersen/Shutterstock, pages 12–13

© Stu Shaw/Shutterstock, page 14
© ChiccoDodiFC/Shutterstock, page 15
© karelnoppe/Shutterstock, pages 16–17
© Felix Mizioznikov/Shutterstock, page 18
© Robert Hoetink/Shutterstock, page 19
© deepspace/Shutterstock, page 20
© smikeymikey1/Shutterstock, page 21
© sirtravelalot/Shutterstock, page 22–23
© Monkey Business Images/Shutterstock, page 24

Design by Interrobang Graphic Design Inc.
Printed and bound in China

We acknowledge the financial support of the Government of Canada.

Firefighters must come to the rescue quickly when there is a fire. They drive trucks called fire engines.

The fire engine carries a powerful hose and a long ladder. It has a siren to use when there is a fire. Have you heard the noise fire engines make?

Firefighters must be strong to carry the heavy equipment and control the powerful fire hoses.

The hose sprays water into the middle of the flames. The firefighters must hold on tightly!

The smoke from a fire can make people sick, so firefighters carry tanks of fresh air to breathe.

This firefighter is trying to put out flames on a roof. He doesn't want the building to burn down. Do you think he will put out the fire in time?

Firefighters make sure everyone is safe. Sometimes firefighters are hurt while helping other people.

Sometimes cars catch fire. Although the fire is small, this firefighter is careful to protect his body with a thick coat.

Look at all the controls on this fire truck! The firefighter knows what each is for.

When there are no fires, firefighters wait at the firehouse. They make sure their equipment is clean and works properly.

FIRE STATION NO. 3

This fire was hard to reach from the ground, so the firefighter sprays water down on it from high above.

Sometimes fires start on boats or ships, or on buildings near the water. Fireboat to the rescue!

Helicopters can dump water over large areas. That's important because forest fires spread quickly.

Small towns use volunteer firefighters. They may be cooks, dentists or librarians, but they all come running when the town siren wails.

This woman knew she wanted to be a firefighter when she was a child. She always feels glad that she is helping people.